bending
becoming

Beth Gwen Hassall

BookLeaf Publishing
India | USA | UK

bending breaking becoming © 2024 Beth Gwen Hassall

All rights reserved.

No part of this publication may be reproduced, stored in a retrieval system, or transmitted, in any form or by any means, electronic, mechanical, photocopying, recording or otherwise, without the prior written permission of the presenters.

Beth Gwen Hassall asserts the moral right to be identified as author of this work.

Presentation by *BookLeaf Publishing*

Web: www.bookleafpub.com

E-mail: info@bookleafpub.com

ISBN: 9789360943370

First edition 2024

The words in this book are dedicated to all of you who have ever felt heartbroken, alone, lost and confused.

To those who weren't convinced things would ever get better.

To those that still aren't.

Keep going.

B x

ACKNOWLEDGEMENT

To every person that has ever had an impact on my life;
good or bad,
big or small.

You've helped me to become the person I am today through these experiences, and for that I am eternally grateful.

It is thanks to every one of you, that I am able to share these poems today (and hopefully help others with them too).

Ours

I've been trying to run away.

From my mind,
from my life,
from my sorrow.

I've been trying to escape.

The pain,
the hurt,
the hollow.

I've been moving from place to place,
in hopes of finding something better.
Somewhere to quiet my mind.
Somewhere with nicer weather.

I thought I could leave my problems.
They didn't need to come with me.
So off I went on a journey,
in hopes of finding a 'better' me.

But what I didn't realise.
What I refused to accept.
Was that no matter where I went,
it was in my mind, the anxieties were kept.

It didn't matter if I ran,
or hid,
or tried to flee.

Everywhere I went,
I was filled with unease.

Because that's the thing with worry,
it follows us around.

It doesn't matter where we are.
Who we're with.
What we're doing.
It will try to keep us down.

We cannot run from it.
We cannot hide, nor flee.
The only thing that really works,
is sitting and let it be.

Once you let it stay a while,
I think it gets a little bored.
It packs its bags,
and off it goes.
Somewhere new to head towards.

It'll come back,
of course it will.
But we will not give it the power;

To make us leave,
a life we love.

For this life,
is ours.

Re-Ignite

We must make the effort to re-ignite the spark.

To find the beauty in everyday; even if some days, we have to look a little harder and dig a little deeper.

Because there is always magic to be felt, and there is always magic to be found.

To those who are open to receiving it, that is.

If you don't believe in luck, then you will never have any.
If you don't believe in love, you will push it away and remain alone.
If you don't believe in miracles, you will never have the honour of experiencing one.

If we want to see the good in this world, then we must be open to it - eyes wide and ears listening.

If we want to experience love, we have to give and receive it freely; with no attachment or expectation.

If we want to be happy, joyous, cheerful - we must choose to be; and release the negative habits, thoughts and emotions weighing us down.

If we want to believe that the glass is half full, then we must first realise...

That we are blessed to have a glass, to call our own, in the first place.

Foolish

But things change,
and people do too.
I was foolish to think,
it would be me and you.

I look back at the memories,
but things just aren't the same.
That's just how life goes,
neither of us are to blame.

I'm grateful for the time we had;
the love and the care.
I just hoped that it would be you,
who would always be there.

My Dear

I used to think,
that there was no 'me' without 'you'.

But now I know,
that there is no me without:

Long walks among the trees
Tangerine skies and glistening stars
Belly laughs with the people who care
Cups of warm tea that fill my soul
And pancakes for dinner (cause' who's gonna stop me?)

I have discovered the truly wonderful things in life.

And you,
my dear,
are not one of them.

Anyway

We get told,
that if someone loves us,
cares for us,
treats us right;

Then we should never let them go.
That we should be sure to 'hold on tight'.

But what if deep down,
we know that they aren't ours to keep.

That someone else could love them more,
love them better,
go head first,
and dive in deep.

Do you stay
in the presence of guilt?

Or leave
and be filled with pain?

Do you try to love them
bigger and better?

Or accept that
there's nothing more to gain?

We get told,
that if we have it good,
we'd be silly not to stay.

But sometimes in your heart,
you know you need go,
anyway.

Temporary

They were never yours to keep;
the places, the people -
they simply belong to themselves.

You were a fortunate passer-by,
who got to experience their beauty,
and create memories that will last a lifetime.

I know now,
that nothing lasts forever.

Most things barely even last a while.

But we learn the lessons,
we treasure the moments,
and we never stop living with love.

Heartbreak

Everyone talks about how much it hurts to get
your heart broken.

But how about when you're the one who's doing
the breaking.

Seeing pain in the eyes of someone you love.
Knowing you caused it.
Knowing you could have prevented it;
but now it's done.

Walking away from someone you adored.
Someone that you really did hope,
would be yours.

You watch their smile fade,
and the pain grows stronger.
You think about the memories;
"Should I have stayed longer?"

I think breaking a heart,
breaks our own heart as well.
"Did I make the right choice?"
Only time will tell.

Bending

Rainy days don't last forever.

Even though sometimes,
it feels like they do.

I promise there will, again, be a time,
where the skies are a wonderful blue.

Healing can feel like a lot like breaking,
like your whole world is falling apart.

But we must remember that this ending,
is opening the door to our new start.

Please don't be scared,
of what you're feeling.
You're not breaking,
only bending.

In the shadows,
and in the dark;
it is to your wounds,
that you are tending.

Perspective

Living life with a grateful heart changes everything.

You start seeing stars,
where before you could only see darkness.

You start smelling beautiful flowers,
inhaling deep breaths of fresh, ocean air.

You start feeling the sun warm your skin,
through the dark and gloomy clouds.

The only change is perspective.

The world around us depends upon how we choose to view it.

But then…

Life is full of surprises.

You think you know what you want.
You think you're on 'the right track'.
You think that everything is falling into place.

But then...

One day,
you're not sure anymore.

You're questioning yourself,
your choices,
your life.

It feels as though it's unravelling at the seams -
but you're not quite quick enough to catch it,
to patch it back up.

You went from everything,
to nothing,
in the blink of an eye.

From understanding,
to questioning,
almost overnight.

What happens now?
How am I supposed to know?
Is it left? Or right?
Where am I supposed to go?

I once felt so certain,
but now I am unsure.

I spend my days worrying.

I don't feel so good anymore.

Glass

It's easy to be happy and grateful,
when everything is going your way.

When your skin is clear,
the sky is blue,
you got something you always wanted.

But it takes bravery and courage,
to find the light in darker times.

When you hate looking in the mirror,
the clouds are hanging over you,
nothing you do feels good enough.

Remember,
we always have a choice,
if the glass is half empty or half full.

Or,
we can choose to be grateful for the fact,
that we have any glass at all.

Happy Again

I feel happy again,
and it feels scary to say;
because what if now,
it gets taken away?

The sky is a bright and blue,
the air is crisp and clear.
My mind is free of worry,
my soul is free of fear.

I hear the birds start singing,
the children begin to laugh.
The knot in my stomach has left,
the feel of sadness - has passed.

My smile is getting bigger,
my eyes are shining bright.
I'm grateful for another day,
after so many dark nights.

Soul Mate

I thought I found my soul mate -
but then it happened again.
They say 'you know when you know',
but how? When?

I thought I found my soul mate,
but I turned and walked away.
They say that if we're meant to be,
we'll meet again one day.

I thought I found my soul mate,
but do they even exist?
Should I stop my search for love?
Or, do I persist?

I thought I found my soul mate,
and maybe I was right.
Maybe you can have more than one.
Maybe some, only last the night.

I think I've found my soul mate,
and I hope this to be true.

Maybe all along,
my soul mate,
was you.

Breathing

They say that home isn't a place,
it's a feeling.

But the problem with feelings,
is that they are fleeting.

I've felt home so many times before,
just to lose it all in a matter of moments.

I tried to hold on to an intangible thing,
and so it left me leaving me hopeless.

I've found home in places,
and I've found home in lovers.

But once you leave,
they make their home in others.

Is it freeing or is it fearful,
to never feel like you are 'home'.

No matter where you are,
a part of you is always gone.

We leave pieces of ourselves,
wherever we go.

We give pieces of our hearts,
to everyone we know.

They say that home isn't a place,
it's a feeling.

I want that feeling so badly.

I crave it every moment I'm breathing.

Proud

I want to reinvent myself,
I want to make a change.

I want to wake up and feel brand new,
to start all over again.

I want to leave the past behind,
to step foot into the new.

I want to be brave and have the courage,
to do as I want to do.

I want to reinvent myself,
I want to make a change.

I want to look back at my life one day,
and be proud of who I became.

Highlight Reel

I see their posts on Instagram,
and my body fills with fear.
"I'll never have what they have",
whilst my eyes fill with tears.

They have the best of everything,
and never seem to be sad.
"Why can't I be like everyone else?"
I say, feeling mad.

But what we tend to forget -
one tiny little detail.

What people post on social media,
is simply a highlight reel.

Unexplained

I've given up trying to understand everything.

Trying to make it all make sense.

Somethings just are,
no rhyme,
no reason,
no brains needing to be wrecked.

It's nice to know,
to understand,
but it's always better to feel.

Que será será.
It is what it is.
Let it just 'be',
so that you can heal.

Growing Pains

You're going to miss the old you,
and how she seemed to shine,
in a way that you feel, you no longer do.

You're going to miss the moments,
and the memories, and people,
that now leave your soul in a dull, painful,
heartache.

You're going to long for the past,
and wish away the nostalgia.

Forgetting that back then,
you were longing for the future.

It's okay to look back fondly,
and it's okay to be sad.

But please don't wish away the magic of life,
right now,
where you are at.

You're not the same, no,
because you have grown.

And you're always going to miss the places and people,
that you once called home.

But the past versions of you,
will forever live on.

And in the memories of others,
you will never be gone.

Growing pains hurt, yes,
but they also heal.

And what a wonderful thing it is,
to have loved,
to have lived,
and to deeply feel.

Milton Keynes UK
Ingram Content Group UK Ltd.
UKHW021102200324
439767UK00016B/624